NORTH AMERICAN
WOLVES

NORTH AMERICAN WOLVES

by Barbara Keevil Parker

A Carolrhoda Nature Watch Book

Carolrhoda Books, Inc. / Minneapolis

To Duane, Stacy, Pam, Jon, Brandon, Makayla, and Alexandra

I thank my family; Ron Martini, Roger Williams Park zookeeper, Providence, RI; Lynn Burkhardt at the Barrington Public Library, RI; and my writer's group for reading a draft of this manuscript and for making helpful suggestions. I also thank Susan Breckner Rose, whose editorial expertise polished the text. And to Sue Behrns, thanks for the tour of the red wolf off-site breeding facility in Graham, WA, a part of Pt. Defiance Zoo, Tacoma, WA.

Carolrhoda Books, Inc.
c/o The Lerner Publishing Group
241 First Avenue North, Minneapolis, MN 55401 U.S.A.
Website address: www.lernerbooks.com

LIBRARY OF CONGRESS CATALOGING-IN-PUBLICATION DATA

Parker, Barbara Keevil.
    North American wolves / by Barbara Keevil Parker.
        p.   cm.
    "A Carolrhoda nature watch book."
    Includes index.
    Summary: Examines the physical characteristics, behavior, and life cycle of the gray wolf and the red wolf.
    ISBN 1-57505-095-1 (alk. paper)
    1. Wolves—Juvenile literature.   2. Red wolf—Juvenile literature.
[1. Red wolf.   2. Wolves.]   I. Title.
QL737.C22P348 1998
599.773—dc21   97–41572

Manufactured in the United States of America
1 2 3 4 5 6 – JR – 03 02 01 00 99 98

Photographs are reproduced through the courtesy of: © Lynn Stone, front cover, pp. 23 (bottom), 39, 45; © Robert Winslow, back cover, pp. 9, 13, 14, 16–17, 25, 28 (top), 29, 36 (right), 37; © Layne Kennedy, pp. 2, 4–5, 8, 11 (left), 15 (bottom), 22, 23 (top); © Thomas Kitchin/Tom Stack and Associates (TSA), pp. 6, 10, 26, 34 (top), 44; Jim Brandenburg–Minden Pictures, pp. 7, 32, 33 (right), 36 (left); Rick McIntyre, pp. 11 (right), 15 (left), 19, 24, 31, 33 (left), 34 (bottom), 35, 42–43; © Frank Staub, p. 18; © John Shaw/TSA, p. 20; © 1997 Michael Evan Sewell, pp. 21, 30; © Jeff Foott/TSA, p. 27; © Victoria Hurst/TSA, p. 28 (bottom); © Robert Winslow/TSA, p. 38; illus. by George Catlin, p. 40; illus. by Walter Crane, from *Little Red Riding Hood,* p. 41.

CONTENTS

THE HUNT

A huge male gray wolf stands alone on a mountain ledge. His eyes scan the landscape for movement. His ears strain forward, listening intently to the sounds of the wilderness. Hunger pains gnaw at his stomach.

The wolf twitches his nose, sniffing the air. The scent of a moose reaches his nostrils. He raises his nose toward the sky and howls. The other wolves resting in a sheltered area below the ridge hear his howl and leap to their feet, joining their leader with howls and yips. The wolves' voices echo against the mountain ridges.

All of a sudden, the wolf pack plunges down the ridge, running swiftly yet quietly, one wolf following another. Entering a meadow, they see the moose. The moose's scent tells the wolves it is old and sick. The pack leader glances at his wolves, signaling them to surround the moose. He waits a moment, then charges at the moose. The pack follows.

The moose faces the attacking gray wolf and slashes at him with its sharp hooves, barely missing the wolf's head. All the wolves pull back and wait.

The moose stands watching the wolves. Suddenly it turns and runs, trying to escape the hungry pack.

Wolves take off after a moose.

After a successful kill, wolves eat their prey. The leader of the pack eats first, and then the rest of the wolves get to eat.

Instantly the gray wolf signals the other wolves to attack. This time, the old moose is not able to defend itself. The wolves jump on the moose with deadly force. The moose falls to the ground. Death comes quickly, and the wolves begin their meal.

The wolf is a **predator**, an animal that hunts and eats other animals. The animals that predators kill and eat are called **prey**. The wolf's usual prey includes moose, elk, bison, and smaller animals. Hunting large animals is difficult, so wolves usually hunt in groups called **packs**. They are most successful at killing the weakest members of a herd of prey animals —the young, old, and sick.

WOLVES AS PREDATORS

Fifteen to thirty million years ago, meat-eating **mammals** known as creodonts hunted prehistoric prey animals. Creodonts **evolved**, or gradually developed, into two groups: catlike animals that sneaked up on their prey and doglike animals that chased their prey. Wolves, coyotes, jackals, and foxes evolved from the doglike animals. Domesticated dogs evolved from the wolf.

Wolves are well equipped for life as predators. Their long, powerful legs and big feet make it possible for them to chase prey for 20 miles (32 km) or more. A wolf chasing its prey runs at 25 to 40 miles per hour (40–64 km/h). That's as fast as a car travels on a city street.

Wolves use their powerful legs to jump across rivers and run long distances.

When a wolf growls, it shows its long, pointed canine teeth.

Wolves' teeth also help them to be successful predators. When Little Red Riding Hood told the wolf he had big teeth, she was right. Wolves' four canine teeth—the sharp, pointed teeth on both sides of the upper and lower jaw—may grow up to 2 inches long (5 cm). Adult wolves have 42 teeth, 10 more than humans. Their jaws are powerful, enabling them to crush bones.

Wolves use their keen senses—hearing, smelling, and seeing—to help find and catch their prey. A wolf turns its ears like radar receivers toward a sound. Their ears hear sounds a human can't hear, including sounds up to 6 miles away (10 km). They can even hear an animal who is buried under the snow. If the wind is right, a wolf's sensitive nose can smell prey a mile or more away.

Wolves see better in dim light than they do in bright light. But even if a wolf cannot tell exactly what is moving, it can see something that is far away.

GRAY WOLVES AND RED WOLVES

North America is home to two kinds, or species, of wolves: the gray wolf *(Canis lupus)* and the red wolf *(Canis rufus)*. Gray wolves also live in parts of Europe, Asia, and the Middle East.

Gray wolves aren't always gray. They can be black, gray, brown, tan, white, or a combination of these colors. Colors are the wolf's **camouflage**. Camouflage helps to keep animals from being noticed by their prey and also hides them from predators, such as human hunters. Gray wolves living in the Arctic are often white, which helps them blend in with the snow.

Most North American gray wolves live in Canada and Alaska, but some live in the northern states of Montana, Wyoming, Idaho, Washington, Minnesota, Wisconsin, and Michigan.

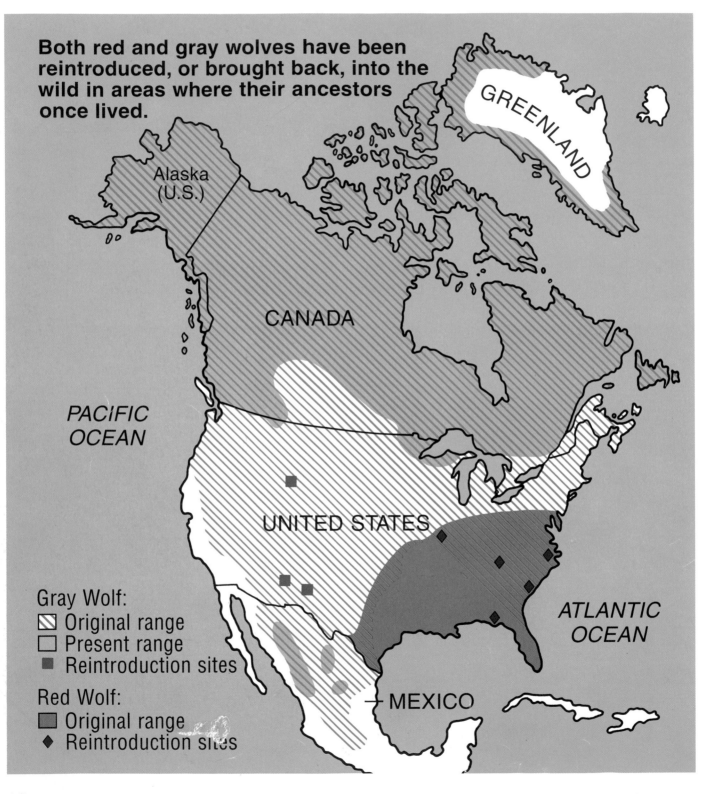

Both red and gray wolves have been reintroduced, or brought back, into the wild in areas where their ancestors once lived.

GREENLAND

Alaska (U.S.)

CANADA

PACIFIC OCEAN

UNITED STATES

ATLANTIC OCEAN

Gray Wolf:
▨ Original range
☐ Present range
■ Reintroduction sites

Red Wolf:
▨ Original range
◆ Reintroduction sites

MEXICO

Gray wolves weigh from 55 to 120 pounds (25–54 kg). Average adult males are 88 pounds (40 kg), and females are 83 pounds (38 kg)—the size of a German shepherd dog or an Alaskan malamute. Wolves living in Alaska, the Yukon Territory, and the Northwest Territories of Canada are usually the largest. The biggest wolf ever caught weighed 175 pounds (79 kg)—that's as much as an average adult man. From nose to tip of tail, gray wolves are 5 to 6 feet long (1.5–1.8 m), and they stand 26 to 32 inches tall (66–81 cm) at the shoulder.

Although there are several subspecies of the gray wolf, the Mexican wolf *(Canis lupus baileyi)* is the smallest member of the gray wolf family. But *el lobo*, as it is called in Spanish, is still an impressive animal. Adults weigh 60 to 90 pounds (27–41 kg) and are 53 to 78 inches long (135–198 cm) from head to tail.

The Mexican wolf is smaller than other gray wolves.

Red wolves look much like coyotes.

Red wolves aren't really red. They are mostly brown with dark guard hairs and light-colored bellies, but they have reddish fur on their heads, ears, and toward the backs of their legs. Red wolves live in the southern United States.

Smaller than gray wolves, red wolves are 4 to 5½ feet long (1.2–1.7 m) and weigh 40 to 80 pounds (18–36 kg). Some scientists think that the red wolf is a cross between the gray wolf and the coyote.

Whether they live in warm or cold climates, wolves have two kinds of fur. Their underfur is thick and woolly and traps heat. In the winter, it can be 2½ inches thick (6.4 cm). When summer comes, the underfur is shed. Over the underfur are long guard hairs. Guard hairs keep the wolf's skin dry. For extra warmth on the coldest days of winter, the wolf curls into a ball, tucks its nose between its hind legs, and covers its face with its bushy tail.

14

Leaving a scent mark of urine, left and below, a wolf shows other wolves the boundaries of its territory.

CATCHING AND KILLING PREY

Each wolf pack, or family, lives and hunts in a territory of its own. Just as dogs wander from tree to fence post to rock, lifting a hind leg and leaving a trace of urine, wolves mark the boundaries of their territory by leaving scent markers of urine and feces on trees, rocks, and piles of dirt. Other wolves who are not members of this pack smell the scent and know they are not welcome. A pack will fight to defend its territory from other wolves. Every few weeks, members of the wolf pack patrol their boundaries to leave fresh scent markers.

A wolf pack's territory ranges in size from 50 to 150 square miles (130–389 km²). Wolves may travel 40 to 60 miles a day (64–97 km) within their territory looking for food. Territories change as the food supply changes. For example, when caribou move north in the summer, the wolves follow.

Wolves must go where they can find a plentiful food supply. If they cannot find food, they will die. A wolf's diet depends on where it lives and the types of animals that also live there. In the Arctic, wolves eat caribou, arctic hares, musk oxen, and Dall sheep. In Minnesota, wolves feed on deer and moose. Red wolves, living in the South, eat rabbits, beaver, and mice. Although wolves will eat whatever small animal they can catch, they prefer to kill a larger animal, such as a moose

or an elk, because it provides them with more meat.

Wolves hunt as a pack. When hunting, the leader of the pack goes first, with the other wolves following behind, usually in single file. Sometimes wolves follow fresh scent trails or come upon their prey accidentally. Other times they catch the scent of their prey as they rest with the pack.

In Yellowstone National Park, a wolf pack hunts in single file.

Wolves usually start their attack by stalking their prey—sneaking as close as possible without being noticed. Suddenly they rush toward it. The sudden rush is meant to frighten the prey, making it run away. Larger prey—moose, elk, caribou, deer, bighorn sheep, bison, or musk oxen—may stand and face the pack. Wolves would rather not attack large, healthy animals that face them because they could be injured by hooves or horns.

A bull moose's enormous antlers can seriously injure a wolf.

The leader of a wolf pack chases an elk.

If the animal runs, the chase begins. The leader, followed by the rest of the pack, begins the chase. Working as a team, some wolves may hold back or circle to wait in ambush. Large prey animals often outrun the wolves. But if the animal gets tired from running or defending itself, the whole pack moves in for the kill. Wolves attack large prey animals by biting high at the rump, flanks, neck, or shoulders. These areas are the safest because they are farthest from the front and hind hooves. Wolves also bite the animal's nose. An animal with a wolf hanging onto its nose will try to get the wolf off and will forget to protect the rest of its body. Then the other wolves can attack with less risk of getting hurt.

The leader of a wolf pack snarls at the other wolves, warning them to back off until it has eaten its fill.

A wolf can eat up to 20 pounds (9 kg) of meat in one meal. Twenty pounds equals 80 quarter-pound hamburgers. If there are leftovers, the wolves often bury some in the ground to be eaten later.

A kill by wolves is celebrated by other woodland creatures. Jays, ravens, small birds, weasels, porcupines, mice, snow-shoe hares, foxes, wolverines, and bears feast on the remains left by the wolves. The wolf is an important part of the food web.

When large prey are hard to come by, wolves will hunt smaller animals—mice, rabbits, and beavers. In the summer, when smaller animals are more plentiful, wolves sometimes hunt alone. The small prey are easier to catch and too small to share with the whole pack.

During the winter, wolves hunt both day and night. In the summer, wolves usually rest during the day when it is hot and hunt after sundown when it cools off.

Wolves help to control the size of animal populations. By attacking prey that are weak, young, or unhealthy, wolves help ensure that the strongest herd animals survive to produce stronger, healthier young. When herds grow too large in numbers, their food supply gets scarce. They eat branches and leaves and bark, leaving behind a dying forest. By helping to keep the size of herds under control, wolves help to save forests and other habitats. By killing diseased animals, wolves help to prevent the spread of disease.

In Alaska's Denali National Park, a wolf finds an arctic ground squirrel for its meal.

FAMILY LIFE

Almost every part of a wolf's life—where it lives, when and how much it eats, whether it will mate—is determined by its pack and its place within the pack. Each wolf has its own place in the pack's **hierarchy**, or social order. The most **dominant** wolves, the leaders, are at the top of the hierarchy. They **dominate**, or guide and control, all the other wolves. The middle-ranked wolves dominate the **subordinate** wolves at the bottom of the hierarchy.

Packs have 2 to 20 wolves. The leaders of each pack are the dominant male, called the **alpha** male and the dominant female, the alpha female. The alpha wolves eat first and choose when to hunt, where to sleep, and the location of the home territory. The alpha wolves lead the hunt and protect the young wolves in the pack from predators. Because they are the senior members of the pack, they have experienced and overcome many dangers.

Below: *A wolf pack is the wolf's family. A dominant wolf stands over a subordinate wolf, right, to show where it belongs in the wolf pack.*

The alpha male reminds two older pups that they are subordinate.

In most packs, the alpha male and alpha female are the only two who mate, and they usually mate for life. When one dies, however, the other wolf may find a new partner. Because the alpha wolves are usually the only wolves to mate, most of the pack are offspring of the alpha pair. Some packs include close relatives of the alpha wolves, such as brothers and sisters. Occasionally another wolf is allowed to join the pack.

The other adult wolves are subordinate to the alphas, but they dominate the younger wolves. Based on personality and size, each wolf establishes its own place in the hierarchy.

Year-old wolves, called yearlings, are as big as adult wolves but are still learning the skills needed to prepare them for adulthood. They are subordinate to the adult wolves. Among themselves, however, the yearlings are still figuring out their place in the pack hierarchy.

The pups are the youngest members of the pack. As they play, they try to discover where they fit in the hierarchy of their age group.

Two wolves fight in order to determine which one is dominant.

Occasionally the wolves in a pack dislike one of the pack members. This wolf, the "scapegoat," is often picked on by the other members of the pack.

Most wolves born to the pack are content to stay with the pack, at least until age two. But because the alpha wolves are usually the only ones to mate, some young adult wolves leave the pack to find a mate or a new pack. These wolves are called lone wolves. If a lone wolf finds a mate, the two wolves start a new pack in a new territory. Some are successful; others remain lone wolves. Many lone wolves do not survive because they do not have a pack to protect them.

25

WOLF TALK

A haunting howl floats across the wilderness. The wolf is not howling at the moon—it howls to communicate with other wolves. Wolves howl to call the pack together, to call for help on a chase, to tell other wolves to stay out of their territory, and to keep in touch with each other when they are separated. Wolves also howl before they go hunting and after a kill. Wolves howl to show happiness at the birth of pups or sadness at the death of a mate. Lone wolves howl to find a mate—the sound leads the two wolves to each other. If the wind is right, wolves can hear howls several miles away. Each wolf makes its own sound. When wolves howl together, they sound like a chorus.

Wolves also talk to each other with other noises. Whimpers show friendliness and **submission**—telling another wolf it is dominant. Pack members whimper when they approach their leader and when they gather as a group. Growling shows aggressiveness and says, "get out of my way," or "beware." Barking usually expresses excitement. Wolves bark while on a chase or as an alarm when other animals come into their territory. Social squeaks are mouselike sounds used when they greet and rub against each other. Squeaks express caring.

Mother wolves use squeaks to talk to their pups.

In addition to sounds, a wolf uses body signals to tell other wolves how it feels. With its face, tail, and stance, a wolf shows its place within the pack hierarchy.

Facial messages express many things, from dominance to submission. A wolf opens its mouth, bares its teeth, wrinkles its forehead, and points its ears forward to show dominance. It shuts its mouth and pulls its ears back and close to its head to show submission.

27

The dominant wolf holds its tail high, while the subordinate wolf tucks its tail between its legs, above. *A subordinate wolf cringes when a dominant wolf growls,* below.

Tails deliver other messages. A tail held high indicates self-confidence. A tail held low or to the side of the body or tucked between the legs shows submission. If a dominant wolf wants to show aggression, it moves the tip of its tail or the whole tail in abrupt twitches. When two wolves of equal rank meet each other, they challenge each other's authority. As they confront each other, their tails are likely to be straight out and trembling. Just like a dog, a wolf shows friendliness with a loose, free, wagging tail.

The rest of the body delivers messages too. To show dominance, a wolf may stand across the front of a wolf who is half lying down. Or a dominant wolf may put its paws across the back of a standing wolf. The wolf on the bottom shows submission. Bristling hair on the back of the neck and rump says, "Back off!" or "Danger!"

A dominant wolf puts both front paws over the back of a subordinate wolf. The subordinate wolf holds its ears back.

Subordinate wolves lick their leader's muzzle to show respect.

Wolves show respect for their leaders by surrounding them, licking their faces, pushing the leaders' muzzles with their noses, or tenderly holding an alpha wolf's muzzle in their mouths without biting. Another way for a wolf to show respect is to move in the direction of an alpha wolf and lift one front paw. Wolf talk is effective. With sounds—whines, growls, squeaks, howls, barks—and body movement—nose pushes and tail wags—wolves express affection and respect for each other and settle disagreements before they become fights.

RAISING PUPS

At the end of winter, the alpha male and the alpha female mate. In the south, this happens as early as late January, while in the north, it can be as late as April. After mating, the alpha female begins looking for a **den** that will shelter her pups. The den is often a hole dug into a hillside or a cave. It may be a place that the pack has used before, or it may be a den deserted by foxes, badgers, or beavers. If the female cannot find a satisfactory den, she digs a new one. The other females of the pack or the alpha male may help with the digging.

An alpha female digs her den.

Ideally, the den has a tunnel leading to a nesting chamber where the pups will be born. The tunnel is narrow so larger animals cannot enter. To prevent the den from being flooded if it rains, the tunnel slants upward and usually turns a corner.

About 63 days after mating—in April, May, or June—the female is ready to give birth. The other wolves in the pack stand outside the tunnel and howl to give her support. The wolves howl, wag their tails, sniff, lick, and dance to celebrate the arrival of the pups. In dancing, they take little tiny steps, bouncing from one foot to another, stomping their feet to show their excitement.

Most **litters,** or groups of young, have 5 or 6 pups. But a litter can have as many as 12 pups. At birth, the pups can't see or hear. They weigh about a pound (.45 kg) and are 8 to 9 inches long (20–23 cm). They have short, pug-nosed snouts and fine woolly hair. After a few days, pups can hear. In 11 to 15 days, they open their eyes. Their eyes are blue at first, but at 3 months, they turn yellow.

Newborn gray wolf pups huddle together in their den.

For the first 2 weeks of their lives, the pups rely on their mother for food and warmth. During this time the mother does not leave her pups. In order for the mother to remain healthy during these 2 weeks, the other members of the pack bring her meat.

The pups **nurse**, or drink from their mother's nipples. Drinking their mother's milk, they gain up to 3 pounds (1.4 kg) a week. As they nurse, the pups struggle for dominance. They all try to get to the pair of nipples closest to their mother's hind legs. Although all the nipples provide milk, the back nipples have the most.

Left: *A three-week-old pup surveys its world through newly opened eyes.*

Newborn pups, **right,** *drink milk from their mother.*

A mother wolf nurses her pups in the shade outside their den, above.
Below: *Seven-week-old pups play with a stick.*

After 2 weeks, the pups can walk, and in about 3 weeks, they come out of the den for the first time. Once the pups leave the den, they pounce on bugs and flowers, wrestle with each other, and sniff whatever is around them. In this way, they develop coordination—they learn to make their feet and legs and body work together. At the same time, they begin to learn about their environment.

The wolf pups play with each other, wrestling to be on top. In their struggle for dominance, their play gets rougher and rougher until one pup gives up and rolls over.

The winner of the wrestling match raises its tail in the air and stands over the loser. The pups continue this fighting until each pup's rank is established from most dominant to most subordinate.

As pups play with each other, they begin to determine where they rank with their littermates.

The whole pack raises the pups. When the mother is ready to hunt again, one of the pack members—an older brother or sister—stays with the pups. The pups begin to develop relationships with all the wolves in the pack. The entire pack will help bring the pups food and defend them, if necessary. The pups learn their place in the pack and how to obey pack leaders from the adults. Pups who misbehave are grabbed by the scruff of the neck and carried away from the pack.

Left: *A pup is carried away from the pack.*
Above: *Pups jump at and lick an older wolf's muzzle.*

A Mexican wolf throws up partly digested meat for her pups to eat.

By around 4 weeks of age, the pups are still too small to follow the pack to the kill, but their teeth are growing and they're ready to eat solid food. So the adult wolves eat at the kill, then return to the pups. The pups crowd around the adults, jumping toward their mouths. When a pup licks the jaws of an adult, the adult arches its back and throws up pieces of partly digested meat. The pup is served a hot meal.

By 8 weeks, the pups have their teeth and no longer need their mother's milk. She weans them by rolling onto her stomach when they try to nurse. The pups are still too young to hunt, but they are also too old for their mother's milk, so pack members bring them chunks of fresh meat to eat. Seeing, tasting, and smelling the meat teaches the pups to recognize the kinds of animals they will hunt someday.

Once the pups can eat meat on their own, the pack moves their meeting place from the den to a **rendezvous site.** The pups stay with an older sibling while the rest of the pack hunts. After hunting, the wolf pack returns to the site, bringing meat to the pups and their older sibling.

As two pups chew on deer bones, they are learning about an animal they will hunt.

The rendezvous site changes throughout the summer as the pack follows its prey. Sometime in the fall, when the pups are ready to hunt, the rendezvous site is abandoned.

Life in the wild is hard. Although wolves in captivity have lived from 17 to 20 years, they are lucky to reach 9 or 10 years of age in the wild. Many wolves just reaching adulthood are wounded by the sharp hooves or horns of their prey. Many have **parasites** infesting their bodies, making them weak or sick. Some develop **rabies** or other diseases that can kill them. Humans—hunters, trappers, ranchers, farmers, and automobile drivers—kill many wolves.

When the pups get old enough, the entire pack moves from the den to a rendezvous site.

WOLVES AND HUMANS

Hundreds of years ago, wolves and humans lived near each other with mutual respect. Native Americans admired the wolf for its loyalty to the pack, its skill at staying hidden, its ability to track, and its use of teamwork to catch prey. As hunters, they imitated many of the wolf's skills.

Shoshone Indians and people in other Western tribes hid like wolves in deep grass and waved wolf tails over their heads to attract curious antelope. Healthy antelope and other herd animals were frightened by people but not by wolves. They knew they could outrun or fend off wolves.

Plains Indians, such as the Pawnee and Sioux, covered themselves with wolf skins. Disguised as wolves, they were able to creep close to bison and other large herd animals.

Although Native Americans sometimes killed wolves for ceremonies or for the warm fur, they had great respect for the wolf. The wolf was considered a symbol of the wilderness, a free spirit. Many Native Americans named themselves after the wolf. In Canada, the Cree Indians believed heavenly wolves visited earth when the Northern Lights shone.

In Europe, people were afraid of the wolf. Europeans were farmers, not hunters and gatherers, and wolves threatened their livestock. Rumors spread that wolves were evil and worthless. Stories were passed from generation to generation about the Big Bad Wolf who tried to eat Little Red Riding Hood and her grandmother, the Three Little Pigs, and Peter and his friends.

Settlers carried the stories told by their European parents and grandparents to North America. They feared the wolf. The settlers created **bounty** laws that rewarded hunters for catching wolves.

As they moved west, the settlers turned the North American prairie into grazing land for their livestock. To put food on their tables, the settlers competed with the wolf for elk, bison, and deer. As the number of prey animals declined, wolves began to feed on livestock. The enraged settlers demanded that the government protect their livestock and wildlife.

Generations of children have heard stories of the Big Bad Wolf, illustrated in 1875 by Walter Crane.

In 1907, the United States government decided to help the settlers by placing a bounty on wolves all over the country. As a result, hunters stalked wolves, hoping to get rich. Most of the wolves were shot, but hunters also used more cruel methods to kill wolves. Painful leg traps and snares snapped wolves' bones. Poison put in dead meat and then eaten by wolves caused them a slow and painful death. Not only did wolves suffer, but the birds and small mammals who feasted on the poisoned meat died as well. Hunters sometimes chased a wolf for sport until it was exhausted, then shot it. Others captured a wolf and wired its mouth shut, which caused it to starve to death.

By 1931 the wolf was nearly **extinct**, without any members of the species still living, in the lower 48 states. Wolves lived in the wild only in Canada, Alaska, and northern Minnesota. In the 1940s, wolves crossed the ice on Lake Superior from Canada to Isle Royale, Michigan, and established a pack there.

In 1973, the Endangered Species Act made it illegal to kill wolves anywhere in the United States except Alaska. Environmentalists watched, hoping wolves would return to the wilderness areas where their ancestors had been slaughtered. In 1979, a gray wolf was spotted after it crossed the Canadian border into Montana. But biologists wanted to build up the wolf population more quickly. In 1995, the U.S. Fish and Wildlife Service rounded up 29 Canadian gray wolves and moved them to central Idaho and to Yellowstone National Park. In 1996, an additional 37 wolves were captured and moved to the same areas. As a result of the work of the Fish and Wildlife Service, gray wolves live in Michigan, Wisconsin, Minnesota, Montana, Wyoming, Idaho, and Washington, in addition to Canada and Alaska. In the late 1990s, plans were underway to return gray wolves to Olympic National Park in Washington.

A pack of wolves, brought into Yellowstone National Park by the U.S. Fish and Wildlife Service, live in the same areas as herds of bison and elk. Here, elk graze high on the hillside, bison rest in the valley, and the wolves run through the middle.

The Mexican wolf once inhabited the Sierra Madre and the surrounding areas in Mexico, Arizona, New Mexico, and Texas. By the 1970s, there were no Mexican wolves living in the United States. The U.S. Fish and Wildlife Service hopes to bring this wolf back to its original southwestern habitat.

For many years, red wolves, extinct in the wild by 1980, could only be found in zoos and wildlife sanctuaries. But in 1987, the red wolf was returned to the wild in North Carolina. By the late 1990s, red wolves lived in North Carolina, South Carolina, Tennessee, Florida, and Mississippi.

Disagreements between farmers, ranchers, hunters, and environmentalists continue to crop up. Some farmers and ranchers fear for their livestock. Some hunters complain that wolves kill the animals that they themselves want to kill for sport. They suggest killing wolves so more game will survive.

In 1982, to calm the fears of livestock owners, the Endangered Species Act was changed to allow U.S. Fish and Wildlife biologists to remove wolves who attack and kill livestock. Ranchers have also been paid for livestock losses. From 1987 to 1997, only 58 cattle and 64 sheep were killed in the northern Rockies. Thirty-eight ranchers were given money for the animals they lost. In 1991, livestock losses in Montana cost $40,000,000. Only $1,250 of those losses were due to wolf kills, far less than expected.

Some people fear wolves, believing they will attack children at the bus stop or kill hikers and skiers. But there has never been a single case of a healthy wolf attacking humans in North America. Wolves are shy and would rather run away from humans.

Wolves will never again roam freely over all of North America. Large cities, roads, and farms limit the space available for wolves. But wolves are adaptable. Given the chance, they will survive. The wolf's future depends on maintaining wilderness areas. There the wolf can live undisturbed. Perhaps one day all major national parks and wilderness areas of the lower 48 states will again echo with the haunting call of the wild, the voices of the pack.

GLOSSARY

alpha: the name given to the male and female leaders of each wolf pack. Alpha is the first letter in the Greek alphabet.

bounty: a fee paid for catching or killing an animal

camouflage: blending in with one's surroundings

den: a warm, safe place such as a hole in the ground or a cave where wolf pups are born and spend the first four weeks of their lives

dominant: the strongest, most powerful, highest ranking member of a group

dominate: to rank higher than another

evolve: a gradual change from its original form to its present form

extinct: when all the animals of a certain species disappear forever

habitat: the kind of environment where an animal lives

hierarchy: the social structure of a wolf pack, based on positions of dominance and subordinance held by the pack members

litter: a group of babies born at one time by one mother

mammals: animals that breathe air, give birth, and produce milk for their young

nurse: to drink mother's milk

pack: a group of wolves, usually related, that live together

parasite: an organism that lives inside an animal and feeds on the animal, usually resulting in harm to the animal

predator: an animal that hunts and kills other animals

prey: animals hunted by other animals for food

rabies: a disease that affects an animal's brain and causes the animal to wander and bite at other animals. It is spread by the bite of an infected animal

rendezvous site: a place where pack members meet between hunting trips and where the pack moves when the pups are old enough to move out of the den

submission: showing weakness or subordinance

subordinate: a less important, lower ranking member of a group

INDEX

ABOUT THE AUTHOR

Barbara Keevil Parker has shared her love and knowledge of wolves through classroom visits and articles for children's magazines. She enjoys observing animals while hiking at Mount Rainier, in Denali National Park, in the woods of New England, or when sitting on the porch in her backyard. A native of Washington State, she now lives in Rhode Island with her husband, Duane. Barbara is a member of the Society of Children's Book Writers and Illustrators. She is also the author of a book on Susan B. Anthony.